A.

GYM

THING

by Tom Vallen

Published by Playdead Press 2018

© Tom Vallen 2018

Tom Gill has asserted his rights under the Copyright, Design and Patents Act, 1988, to be identified as the author of this work.

A CIP catalogue record for this book is available from the British Library.

ISBN 978-1-910067-64-2

Playdead Press
www.playdeadpress.com

A GYM THING

by Tom Vallen

A Gym Thing premiered on 2nd August 2017 at The Pleasance Courtyard, Edinburgh Festival with the following cast:

Will Shaw	Tom Vallen
Jay Witter / Damon Collins	Tarrick Benham
Rebecca Harrison	Bethan James
Director	Philip Scott-Wallace

This playtext was published for the London transfer, 30th April 2018 at The Pleasance Theatre, with the following cast:

Will Shaw	Tom Vallen
Jay Witter / Damon Collins	Gabriel Akuwudike
Rebecca Harrison	Jennifer Brooke
Director	Philip Scott-Wallace
Sound Designer	Adam Welsh
Lighting Designer/Operator	Saulius Valiunas
Dramaturge	Philip Scott-Wallace
Photography Credit	Sally Jubb Photography
Pr	Chloe Nelkin Consulting
Producers:	Tom Vallen (Working Cast Productions)
	Philip Scott-Wallace (Small Things Theatre)

Working Cast is an actors only staffing agency which uses company profit to promote and produce it's actors work. *A Gym Thing* is Working Cast Production's London theatre debut.

Small Things Theatre stage exceptional productions that champion writers, performers and creatives from the fringe to the west end. Their regular Night Of Small Things collaborates with playwrights, actors, musicians, comedians and poets to provide a platform for established and emerging artists to come together to experiment and showcase their work. They also work in education and events.

This production has kindly been supported by The Body Dysmorphic Disorder Foundation.

CAST

TOM VALLEN
Writer / Producer / Will Shaw

A Gym Thing is Tom's debut piece of writing. As an actor theatre credits include: *Bash* by Neil LaBute (Old Red Lion/ Trafalgar Studios) and *A Gym Thing* (Pleasance Courtyard, Edinburgh). TV credits include: *Episodes* (BBC / Showtime), *Casualty* (BBC) and *Doctors* (BBC). Radio credits include: *Tommies* (BBC Radio 4). Tom is the Artistic Director of Working Cast Productions and is delighted to be bringing the production to London.

JENNIFER BROOKE
Rebecca Harrison

Jennifer trained at Italia Conti Academy of Theatre Arts.

TV credits include: *White Gold* Series 1 & 2 (BBC Two/Fudge Park); Rachel Hardy in *Hollyoaks* (Channel 4/Lime Pictures. Film credits include: *My Name Is Lenny* (Salon Pictures); *Astral* (Craven Street Productions.) Theatre credits whilst training include: *Touched; The Children's Hour; The Other Woman in Two; On The Shore of The Wide World; Richard III; A View From The Bridge; The Acid Test.*

GABRIEL AKUWUDIKE
Jay Witter / Damon Collins

Gabriel trained at Drama Centre London.

Television includes: *The Bisexual* (Channel4/Hulu), *Informer* (Neal Street Productions/BBC). Theatre includes: *No One Is An Island* (Tangle Theatre), *Troilus & Cressida* (Sam Wanamaker Festival 2017 Shakespeare's Globe), *Mary Barnes, The Caucasion Chalk Circle, As You Like It, Pretend It Away, Tartuffe and The Cherry Orchard* (all for Drama Çentre). Film includes: *X21* (The Wholls music video)

CREATIVE

PHILIP SCOTT-WALLACE
Director/Producer

Philip is co-artistic director and producer for Small Things Theatre. He is also a director and actor. *A Gym Thing* was his directorial debut and he is delighted to remount the production in London. As a producer his work includes *The Stolen Inches, No Place For A Woman, Anything is Possible If You Think About It Hard Enough* and *Boots* as well as curating events for UN Women's *HeForShe* campaign for gender equality.

ADAM WELSH
Sound Designer

Adam is a sound designer, theatre maker and performer. He has worked internationally, regionally and on London's West End. Notable work includes performing in the original West End cast of *Dreamboats and Petticoats*, *War Horse* in the West End, touring with Headlong Theatre in Anya Reiss's *Spring Awakening* and appearing in *The Silver Tassie for Druid* at the Lincoln Centre Festival in New York. He is an associate artist and founder member of the multi award winning theatre company Dead Centre, who have received international acclaim for their work. Other companies he has worked with include the Royal National Theatre, Barbican, the Schaubühne (Berlin), Druid, Live Theatre, Young Vic, Sage Gateshead, Nuffield Theatre, Bill Kenwright Ltd, The Yard and BAC. For his sound design, he received an Irish Times Theatre Award nomination in 2014. He is currently working on an EP to be released later this year.

SAULIUS VALIUNAS
Lighting Designer / Operator

Theatre includes: *The Observatory* (Vault Festival 2015); *Spelling Bee* (Kraine Theatre, New York); *Boys*, (Vault Festival 2018); *X-NN: Meet Market*, (Vault Festival 2018).

The play wouldn't have reached this stage had it not been for the following people.

Amoreena Campbell at The Body Dysmorphic Disorder Foundation.

All the team at the Pleasance Theatre Edinburgh and London.

Tarrick Benham and Bethan James, thanks for the memories and for believing in the piece.

Cordelia O'Neill, I am forever in awe of your talent and kindness.

Philip Scott-Wallace, thank you for the hours of guidance and mentoring but above all your loyal friendship.

Caroline and Paul Gunnell, excellent flapjack.

Most importantly Mum, Dad and Jo. My dream team.

CHARACTERS

WILL SHAW

25.　　　Painter and Decorator by profession but looking for his true calling. Excellent physical shape. Think Cross Fit muscle composition and stamina. Likeable, middle class and self-deprecating. Will is an over thinker. Passionate.

JAY WITTER

26.　　　London Born. Cheeky and confident. Struggled in school but through no fault of trying to be a friend to all. Estate agent.

REBECCA HARRISON (BEC)

24.　　　Finance Graduate. Bec has a vitality about her that is eye catching. Soft faced but an inner strength that keeps suitors in their place.

DAMON COLLINS

27.　　　Professional. On a finance grad scheme in the City. Book smart, publicly schooled with all it's glory.

The role of Jay and Damon, should be doubled by the same actor.

NOTES

[…]   Indicates a break in the speech but a continuation of internal dialogue. The character either can't, won't or is struggling with what to say.

[/]   Indicates the point of interruption or an overlap in the dialogue.

[-] Indicates the moving on of a thought at a pace or coming in promptly on someone else's.

Lighting: Changes in tense & location, should be hinted at with a shift in lighting.

Notes on movement: The actor playing Will must have a standard of fitness higher than the average gym goer. The plays attraction comes in the Characters athletic ability to undertake strenuous and complex workouts, whilst delivering dialogue with control and pace.

With the possibility of an 8 show week. The movement / exercises should be altered to always show the character working to his absolute maximum. How often the muscle groups need to be rotated will depend on the performers fitness or injuries.

Unless specifically stated the actor should plot out their own workout journey. Always pushing himself. Always impressively athletic and strong.

A Gym Thing - A One Act Play.

Lights snap up on Will.

Charged.

WILL   I didn't think I'd have time, things proper kicked off in the kitchen when cleaning down.

Big breath out. Controlled.

> But it's all good. I'm here now. The hour of the day which is mine, mine to do as I please, mine to sweat out the days thoughts and feelings, shred my skin-shred my fibres. My hour when I don't mind being watched from all angles.

Will clocks the corners of the room.

> An hour no one can take away from me.

Will lifts his top to assess his abs.

> My mate Jay's swinging by soon. Got to look my best.

Will lowers his top with a smile.

> I know that you don't get this, but some, that like Jay and I function with this drug, this addiction that takes over you. They'd know how I'm feeling right now- post shit day- pre workout. Really it's fine if you don't, if it doesn't grab you and get under your skin. It never did me before... I thought, look at them meat heads- them twats- these obsessives just showing off.

11

I couldn't see the point!

Jay Enters.

Will's sat playing playstation, very subdued.

JAY   I've got this offer through work-

WILL   ...

JAY   It's only £15.99 a month when you sign up with a friend.

WILL   Only hey.

JAY   Reload. Mate, you'll love it, it's got swimming and everything.

WILL   Public pools are full of athletes foot, piss and pubes.

JAY   Nah not here. Come on it's beautiful outside let's get you off the couch.

(*Quietly*)

Your Mum will be fine for a few hours.

WILL   ...

JAY   It's not competitive!

(*Playful*)

You could do with cutting in a bit, Summers approaching /

WILL   Don't.

JAY   The woman though! I'm telling-

Will rolls his eyes

It's not the only reason.

Will flicks him a look

Did you see Becca Harrison's back from uni? Her and Carly have Pilates tomorrow morning.

Are you painting tomorrow?

WILL   No.

JAY   Then do a free trial!

Will doesn't respond

You're coming with me.

Jay Exits.

Will starts his stop watch. He rolls his shoulders and warms up his joints.

WILL   Yeah Jay, him that got me into it. Maybe I should pin all this on him.

He always has got his own way. I'll give him that one though, despondent with occasional outbreaks of desolate, I forecasted nothing bright in my path.

Anyway enough chatter. You really want to learn about this? Alright. Well you might want to take your notepad and pen out, I'll be charging you for the next one.

Sleep is vital to performance and recovery, so before lights up you need to have had a solid eight hours.

Pre workout is now whatever you can get, so today was another mug of coffee and a banana, done.

Now's the time to clear your mind, settle in and-focus! For 60 minutes of concentration and application.

Don't worry nobody ever post workout has said "I wish I didn't do that", "Well that was a waste of time". Believe it or not though, 2 years back all this sounded like hell, why would anyone choose to spend an hour stuck in a windowless room getting hot and sweaty?

I just hadn't found my motivation yet.

Bec Enters.

Will steps into the path of Bec.

BEC	Sorry.
WILL	(*Alarmed, shy.*) Rebecca.
BEC	...William. God long time, how are you?
WILL	I'm good...
BEC	...What are you doing?
WILL	Gyming with Jay.
BEC	I meant with yourself, working or... Are you still local?

WILL   Oh, yeah working and just on Hawkins.

BEC   With your Mum?

WILL   Yeah. You?

BEC   Finished Uni /

WILL   Accountant.

BEC   Good memory! Well I'm not chartered but looking for work in that field or anything to be honest. It's nice to see you, send my love to your Mum.

WILL   Yeah you too.

Neither leave.

BEC   Waiting for Carly.

Will twigs why Jay is late.

                Pilates virgin.

WILL   Pilates is good, good, good fun.

Silence.

BEC   Maybe she's inside.

Bec makes to leave. Will waves.

WILL   Enjoy. It's a lovely place... it's got like swimming and everything.

Bec Exits.

WILL   Our only previous was at a year nine disco, I carefully timed it to sit between her legs during oops upside your head.

Jay had landed me right back in it. It'd been eight years since P.E. So the gym! Where do you start? I didn't even own any shorts!

Jay Enters.

Will awkwardly watches Jay undertake a one rep max squat in the rack with a louder than necessary grunt.

JAY   ARGHHHHHHH.

He re-racks the bar and jumps shaking it out.

WILL   Right. What do I do? And don't say 'that'.

Jay pretends to shadow box Will.

JAY   (*Elated*) Becca Harrison hey! Knew you had a soft spot for her.

WILL   I don't deny you played it well. Well done. Now let's not let this take any longer than necessary.

JAY   I'm telling you mate, you're gonna love it! Right some basics. 1) Always replace your equipment. 2) If you can't keep your form, lower the weight. 3) Wipe your sweat off the seats and most importantly, 4) Always be the hardest worker in the room.

Jay slaps Wills bum.

WILL   That's a quote from The Rock isn't it?

JAY	Yeah. Right come on, let's get the heartbeat going.
WILL	Increasing your BP gets vital oxygen to your muscles... we don't want anyone getting hurt now do we?
	On exiting Jay convinced me to sign up, you could cancel anytime so I never felt trapped.

Bec Enters.

	I wanted to triple check that this wasn't for me.
	Pilates was Mondays, Wednesdays and Fridays and I never missed a day.
JAY	Monday, traps.

Will and Jay both do shoulder shrugs. Will's face scrunching with each rep.

WILL	Bec. Bec, Becca... Rebecca, Bec Becca, Bec!

Bec Exits.

WILL	She loved her music.
JAY	Wednesday, squats.

Will attempts to keep up with Jay's squat walks.

Bec enters with her water bottle, Will breaks away Bambi legged to the water fountain. His voice breaks.

WILL	Water.
BEC	Sorry?

WILL	It's good isn't it? (Rambling) I think they should put some Robinson's in the tank so that it pushes out orange squash- not the double strength one though, you always use too much of that, even if you only use a tiny bit it's always way way way too strong.
BEC	I'm pretty sure this won't be coming from a tank.
WILL	Not one for the Dragons Den then?
JAY	FEEL THE BURN!
BEC	(*In a Scottish accent*) "I'm definitely out." Bye Will.

Bec Exits.

JAY	Friday, chest.

Jay assists Will to squeeze out one last rep.

WILL	Yours.
JAY	It's yours.

Bec Enters.

Alternate the following.

WILL	Take it- take it- take it- take it.
JAY	Yours- yours- yours- yours.

Will completes the rep, then struggles to compose himself in front of Bec.

JAY	Go on then.

Will crosses to Bec.

WILL   Congratulations on passing your test. I saw the P on your bumper.

BEC   Oh, good spot. Dad won't let me take it off, 5th times a charm, better late than never.

WILL   Well they say those who pass second time are better drivers anyway, so that makes you three times better than them!

BEC   Every time I've come you've been here. You've never struck me as much of a gym bunny, but I think it suits you.

WILL   Well... I mean I... love to lift.

BEC   Maybe you could show me sometime.

Bec Exits.

WILL   Surprisingly it was, alright. Took me a few visits to build some confidence but I soon learnt my cables from my kettle bells.

          I'd struggled to find my "calling" post college, I knew I didn't want to leave my Mum, and Dad used to be a painter and decorator so I just fell in to that. Shame... engineering would've been proper cool.

          Exploring how buildings withstand pressure, the hydraulics of a lift.

          But now with the gym I'd found it, I'd energy, targets- a sense of place. I loved it.

Right that's pulse raisers complete and a gentle buzz from your pre workout.

Dynamic stretches; proven to improve your range of motion, enhancing your muscular performance and power.

Will double knots his shoes.

And helps you tie your laces.

Next select your song, to start with you don't want anything too heavy, I save Eminem for when things get sweaty. Something nice and upbeat.

Will sings 'Treasure' by Bruno Mars.

"Treasure, that is what you are, honey you're my golden star, you know you can make my wish come true, if you let me treasure you."

His smile fades to something deeper.

Absolute tune no? Always on repeat.

Bec Enters.

BEC   Favourite cheese?

WILL   Brie.

BEC   Stilton.

WILL   Ugh Blue, I wondered what that smell was!

BEC   Very funny.

WILL   Now show me yours.

20

Bec positions herself in a monkey squat.

> Fresh Prince or Simpsons?

BEC Fresh Prince.

Will repositions Bec's hips.

WILL Deal or No Deal, roll your hips more- that's it, or Countdown?

BEC Countdown.

WILL Agreed. I'm well quick at the numbers round. I'd definitely beat you.

Bec stands up straight.

BEC Really? It took you a month to get my number.

WILL Yeah... well, kept you waiting didn't I. Did I say we'd finished?

Bec resumes the squat position.

> Hold it there. Celebrity crush?

BEC Ooooh... Brad Pit in Fight Club.

WILL Oh how I wonder why!

Will correctly positions her back.

> This will take the pressure off your lower back.
>
> Interesting fact?

BEC	Um... I know. If you breath on your hand it's hot air, but if you blow on your hand it's cold air.

Will tries this out.

WILL	Completely useless, but moderately interesting none the less. Perfect, now lead with the top of your head and you'll rise safely.
BEC	Amazing. Favourite song?
WILL	Treasure.
BEC	Shut up! Bruno Mars? That is such a tune.
	Favourite food?
WILL	Curry- no Chinese!
BEC	Yum, tonight?
WILL	Definitely.

Bec Exits.

Chatting absolute crap. Is that not just the best thing in the whole world, the early stages of dating, full of boozy nights, micky taking and making in-jokes. The building blocks for love.

Takes off his jacket to reveal a vest.

Vest wanker I know.

Jay Enters.

Jay quickly showed me there is so much more to your gym life than working out. You've got training plans, apparel, supplements and especially meal prep; you've heard that ab's are made in the kitchen right? /

Jay throws Will a pack of Turkey.

JAY   Heads!

Will examines the products nutritional content.

WILL   18 grams.

JAY   You should have about 1 and a half grams per KG. How much do you weigh?

WILL   About 80, so what's that?

Will and Jay struggle.

                  ...120 grams a day?

Faux confidence.

JAY   At least!

WILL   I also read within 15 minutes of exercise I need to be consuming nearly 20 grams to get the most from what I've just done.

JAY   Here's a shaker, we'll get you some powder, it's easier to consume.

WILL   Thanks mate. Let me know what I owe you.

JAY   On me, I know you've not been busy.

WILL   Ledge.

Jay takes a moment.

JAY   Will… come here a sec. So you know, this is by no means a snap decision.

WILL   Right.

JAY   I've given it quite a bit of thought and I just don't know what people are gonna think. So I wanted you to know first.

Will joins Jay, sensing the seriousness of his tone.

WILL   Okay, alright… well you know you can tell me anything. What is it?

JAY   I'm going to shave my chest.

Will laughs and breaks away.

WILL   Why are you gonna do that?

JAY   Better definition, low cut V, pumped chest, they'll love it.

WILL   You mean Carly will?

JAY   She wants to see me all the time, it's proper intense.

WILL   You were mad about her last week. She's a nice girl mate, and you're an ugly bastard so don't be aiming too high.

Jay pretends to go to hit Will.

          Saturday night's temptations bringing all this on? /

JAY   You didn't see anything.

WILL	(*Hands up surrendering.*) What was there to see? We had a Fifa night didn't we?
JAY	Becca Harrison. 17 year old you is having a wet dream right now.
WILL	Yeah I'm feeling pretty good.
JAY	Keep at it, Bec's had the best.

Jay Exits.

WILL	I was head over heels and I knew Bec deserved the best.
	Right, you ready? I'm going to take you through the whole body.
	Bec was the first girl I'd really fallen for. Everyone remembers them butterflies right? With only a smile she had this angelic ability to turn even the dullest of moments into something from a film. Me, Will Shaw, dating Becca Harrison!
	Like me she's a real work horse my Bec. While most crave a lie in and morning TV, for Bec a month of job hunting and close calls was beginning to take it's toll. She was hungry to get stuck in.

Bec enters, returning from the restaurant toilet.

BEC	Another bottle?
WILL	Yeah.
BEC	I've applications to do.

WILL	You've got all day.
BEC	Will!
WILL	Relax, your degree won't expire.
BEC	This is key Grad intake period. I don't want to be left with the dregs.

Will references the new bottle.

WILL	Perfect then?
BEC	Corny. The industry's packed with nepotism though.
WILL	What's that?
BEC	Parents helping out their kids.
WILL	Right. Shall we get dessert? I might get some Ice cream.
BEC	Ooooh what would Jay say?
WILL	Cheat day.
BEC	As kids whenever we heard the Ice cream van jingle go past, it was really disappointing.
WILL	Were you not allowed Ice cream?
BEC	No. My Dad told my brother and I that if the tune was playing it meant they'd ran out.

They both laugh.

WILL	Could your Dad help?
BEC	No, but Damon's been great.

WILL	Damon, remind me?
BEC	Year above at Leeds, same course. Fast track grad scheme, RBS?
WILL	Yes yes, go.
BEC	He proofs every application for me which is so sweet, his year had it easy though.
WILL	Why?
BEC	Doesn't matter.
WILL	But isn't your Dad like famous?
BEC	No. Well he played number eight for Harlequins and England.
WILL	Oh... ok, nice.
BEC	It's refreshing for you not to know what his exact conversion rate was or tackles made in the blah blah.
WILL	Well if it's refreshing, I've not a clue what a No.8 is or who Harlequins are.
BEC	I'm sure he'll educate you.

Beat.

	Damon did mention something.
WILL	Yeah?
BEC	Someone's retiring and he's hopeful to get me an interview. He's like that with his boss so... It's way above my experience though so I'd

have to seriously impress. Apparently he'd "rather a hole in the office than an arsehole."

WILL   Well you're definitely not that?

BEC   I've literally spoken all night about this haven't I?

WILL   That's ok, it's on your mind. If there's anything I can help with.

BEC   No you're busy finding your own work.

WILL   Don't worry about me, I've as much as I want. When you get this new job, who knows when we'll get nights like this.

BEC   They'll always be time for red wine and Ice cream.

Bec kisses him on the lips.

Bec Exits.

WILL   I'd make a good number eight now.

That Summer Jay convinced me to rent a flat with him closer to our gym in Acton. Mum said she didn't mind and it meant Bec could stay over more.

She landed that role in the City so I mainly used the branch near her work. Exercise was no longer her "priority", but I couldn't get enough of it, surprising really because growing up exercise just wasn't for me, I was more your Warhammer and Scouts kind of kid.

No wonder I got bullied!

Well I didn't get it as bad as some, maybe because my Mum taught at the school. Mrs Shaw, or as the kids liked to call her, "Mrs sure does love it up the arse- in the mouth- on her tits, as a shampoo or toothpaste!" You can't knock their imaginations.

I tried out the odd sport and table tennis became the one for me, 2nd best player in Year 10 after Bodie Carter. So as you can imagine with a tag like that. Absolute babe magnet!

Sometimes though, placing second isn't enough.

Damon Enters.

Will is shaking a protein shake. Damon cautiously approaches Will.

DAMON   Will?

WILL   Yeah.

DAMON   Damon. Rebecca's colleague, she'll be down in 5.

WILL   Oh mate, guy from Leeds yeah?

They shake hands… for a tad too long.

Nice to put a face to a name.

DAMON   You've alot to celebrate /

WILL   Bec said you had a bit to do with her getting the job, thanks, that's really sound of you, I know she's enjoying it.

29

DAMON   Not for you to thank me, Bec got it off her own merit, she'll be chasing me up the ladder in no time.

WILL   Thanks though, I owe you one.

DAMON   Really. You don't.

WILL   You've just moved haven't you?

DAMON   Yeah. Wow. So stressful, I've been making trip after trip, Stratford to Hammersmith, Hammersmith to Stratford, Stratford to Hammersmith, Hammersmith then Stratford, driving me mad!

WILL   What made you choose Clapham?

DAMON   Oh, no no! I've moved to Hammersmith.

WILL   ...Nice!

DAMON   The rents have moved to France so letting me dwell in the family home for nothing. Can't grumble.

Bec Enters.

Here she is, the superstar. Have you told him yet?

Bec completed her probation period! To quote "She satisfies the hole you've all been trying to fill."

Will embraces Bec.

WILL   Amazing / babe.

BEC	He really didn't trigger.
DAMON	Your face was a picture.
BEC	Well you've clearly introduced yourselves.
DAMON	Indeed, best of chums. I was telling Will about Mummy and Dad gallivanting off to Bordeaux.
BEC	C'est merveilleux, je suis très jaloux!
DAMON	Très Bien! Tu parle Francais?
BEC	Je parle un peu le Français.
DAMON	Box of surprises this one. Anyway enough about me, Bec says you've started training for something?
WILL	Really? No.
DAMON	I'd like to do 'The Gym'.
WILL	Why don't you then?
DAMON	Oh God, not enough time.
WILL	Well you make time, an hour's less than 4% of your day.
BEC	Watch out, he'll make you join his cult.
DAMON	I don't think I'd suit it anyhow, all the men with veiny arms, eating chicken and drinking their hulk juice.

Damon notices Will's shake.

	Anyway, don't mind me. You must have somewhere exciting to go with such cracking news.
BEC	Pizza Express, our favourite. Why don't you come with us?
DAMON	No, no.
BEC	No definitely. Come along, we want you too. Will?
WILL	Absolutely.
DAMON	(*Touched by the gesture.*) Ok, well in that case, let me slip into something a little more relaxed and I'll be back with you before the bubbles have settled. And don't you worry, they'll be on me.

Damon Exits.

WILL	Why does your girlfriend always have to have that friend? Good looking fella he was too.
BEC	Do you mind?
WILL	Nah it's fine, nice guy. As long as I get you to myself tonight.
BEC	Can you stay at mine?
WILL	I've AM cardio with Jay.
BEC	Ick ack ock?
WILL	What?

Bec does the hand signals.

BEC   Ick ack ock?

WILL   You mean, rock paper scissors?

BEC   Yeah? Ick ack ock, rock paper scissors. You've never heard of that?

WILL   It's rock paper scissors!

BEC   Ok! Draw after 3. 1.2.3 draw.

Will wins.

BEC   Yours it is then! You're lucky I'd already packed my stuff. Let's go.

Bec Exits.

Jay enters acknowledging the other gym goers.

WILL   Jay and I trained together whenever we could, chasing bigger gains from bigger pumps. Sorry, THE PUMP! It's the feeling of your muscles ripping out of your skin, while the blood smashes through your veins. It's like trying on a jacket a size too small for you, you know it doesn't fit properly but you kinda like it.

                 Nothing compares to that first one.

Will does exactly as Jay says.

JAY   Arm's in to keep your form. Too high a rep and you'll tire, too high a weight and you'll lose the range of movement. You've got to get it just right.

WILL   Your arms shake.

JAY	Teeth locked.
WILL	You plant your feet hoping your roots will feed you with energy, as you /
JAY	Raise the bar /
WILL	One /
JAY	last /

Shaking, an explosion of pleasure and pain.

WILL/JAY	TIME!
WILL	The weights drop to the floor, your arms pulsating in utter ecstasy!

Will comes back around.

> There is something sacred about the relationship with your gym partner, they'll push you till you can't walk, then beast you till you can't crawl, but you love them for it.
>
> I had a world class one in Jay.

Jay is beneath Will holding onto his ankles, Will throws his legs down to the floor.

WILL	10, 9, we need to be separating our workouts, 8, doing chest and tri's- then bi's and back will keep it muscle group specific, getting us bigger pumps.
JAY	(*Agonised*) How many?
WILL	(*Unsure*) 4.
JAY	And legs, it's like holding onto some string.

WILL   And 1.

JAY   Bloody hell.

Jay rolls to his feet, uncomfortable.

Go on then.

They switch positions.

15, 14, these new trainers?

WILL   Yeah, alright aren't they?

JAY   12, 11.

WILL   I've got a new plan for us Monday. 6 weeks.

JAY   9.

WILL   2 weeks 12 reps, 2 weeks 10 reps, 2 weeks 8 reps.

JAY   6.

WILL   Increasing the weight every two weeks, will activate growth and strength.

JAY   The trainer becomes the trainee! I'll take your tips when you can squat a hundred. 4, 3, 3, 4, 2, 2, and 1.

Jay is itching his chest.

JAY   Three months of this mate. Second time I've shaved it back.

WILL   Wax it, actually your birthday's coming up, get an epilator. I can ask Mum to give you some advice.

JAY	How is your Mum?
WILL	Fine.
JAY	And Dad?
WILL	Fine!

Will flex's his bi-cep.

JAY	You're looking good mate, lean.
WILL	Lean? I've put on two centimetres.
JAY	I'm saying you look healthy! I bet Bec's enjoying it?

Will resumes plank position.

WILL	Come on!

Jay tries to join in the plank but fails.

WILL	She hasn't really said. And up, 10 of these.

Side plank, pulsing.

JAY	They all do mate. Fitter the better. Shame you've settled down so quickly, not been able to sample the fruits of your labour.
WILL	Don't talk like that.
JAY	You're missing out.
WILL	Having to jump from shadow to shadow like you, no thanks and switch.
JAY	There's only a shadow if someone shines a light son.

36

WILL   I somehow feel Carly's scrambling for the torch.

JAY   What she doesn't know won't hurt her /

WILL   Don't be a dick.

JAY   Fifa night remember?

Will ignores Jay.

WILL   And plank.

Jay falls flat.

JAY   I'm done. Dinners waiting.

Jay Exits.

Will does a flurry of press ups.

WILL   Fitter the better, fitter... the better.

Bolts to his feet.

I wonder why she put up with him?

For Bec and I, late night incentivised revision sessions in the run up to Christmas, meant bleary eyed frosty morning sprints to work became the norm. Staying together was the best, that comforting thought that every night you get into bed with the one you love made every session worth it.

And lean... dickhead.

Will tries to examine the condition of his back and twinges his neck. Bec enters and starts massaging it. Will is in great discomfort.

BEC	This can't be good for you?
WILL	Ahhhhh it is, I just didn't warm up properly. Softer!
BEC	It looks like it. What were you doing?
WILL	Shoulder shrugs.
BEC	You need to rest.
WILL	No it just needs releasing. I've changed program. I've been told I should be lifting as heavy as possible to build up my strength.
BEC	Well don't injure yourself or you won't be able to paint.
WILL	Ahh just there.

Painful chuckles.

BEC	I had my exam.
WILL	Oh my God, sorry, how was it? Did you smash it?
BEC	I don't know.
WILL	What was it?
BEC	Governance, risk and ethics.
WILL	Yes! Yes. I bet you aced it.
BEC	I don't know. I'm against Oxbridge grads and I don't want to let Damon down.
WILL	Bit harder. You should start back at the gym, release some stress.

BEC	Only guy I know who'd recommend the gym as the go to stress release.
WILL	Don't be jealous.
BEC	I get my results on Wednesday, providing it goes well I thought we could go out for the evening?
WILL	Sure, I'm going to a body expo in the day, but I'll come after?
BEC	I'd love that. I got you a little prezzie today.
WILL	Really?

In the excitement Will twinges his neck.

BEC	It's only small /
WILL	Some scales! Bec this is awesome. You didn't have to get me this.
BEC	I have to make an effort, the gyms like some slutty mistress I'm having to compete with.
WILL	You know this is all for you.

Will strikes a pose which makes them both laugh.

	Why don't I make us some protein flapjack?
BEC	Yum.
WILL	I love you.
BEC	I love you too.

Bec Exits.

WILL   There's nothing more rewarding than seeing results.

Jay enters steaming.

Jay conveniently noticed I hadn't been out for a few weeks and as usual was desperate to get on it whilst Carly was away. But this time I thought, why not? I had a lot to celebrate. Nothing that crazy though.

As for Jay, what is it they say? A couple of drinks loosens the tongue? Well add in to that a bag of whiff, a twenty pack of Camel Blue and he spouts off like he's fucking Pinnochio.

JAY   It's too soon!

WILL   Thanks.

JAY   I don't want to piss on your bombfire but you've been dating what, five months? Na. No way. Nada.

WILL   Because you know what love is don't you?

JAY   You like her because she's fit.

Sings out of tune.

"*Loving you is easy 'cause you're beautiful.*"

WILL   Let me just Shazam that one.

JAY   Minnie Riperton mate. Classic.

WILL   Is that Tequila?

JAY	Yeah, little trick for you, it's the same as celery, you lose weight.
WILL	That isn't true.
JAY	How do you know she isn't nailing her work mate?
WILL	What Damon? No way.
JAY	You wanna bang him out.
WILL	Why?
JAY	Snooping round ya bird, chat shit get banged.
WILL	Chat shit? /
JAY	Chat shit get banged!
WILL	You've some lovely views on relationships, maybe write them down and have a little read in the morning.
JAY	What you saying?
WILL	Nothing.

Beat.

	Where does Carly think you're right now?
JAY	She's away with work.
WILL	Right!
JAY	Oh shut up. Boys night out!

WILL	You run to me every time you can to have a blow out, then she blames me when she can't get hold of you.
JAY	What she doesn't know won't hurt her.
WILL	It will do.
JAY	(*Childishly*) Oh my names Will, I've had sex with two woman in my life and now I'm going to get married.
	You lift a few weights and suddenly you think you're Billy big balls.
WILL	So you're going to continue?
JAY	We're not designed to just be with one person. Come back to me when you've felt the rush of trying to hit the magic seven.
Clarifies	
	A different girl every night! Think of this as my extended gap year, I'm exploring the world between my 4 bed posts.
WILL	That's not cool.
JAY	Keep lifting mate. You'll get there.
Jay Exits.	
WILL	I am getting there!
	We've all got that one mate who goes a bit weird when loving the sesh. I've lost the love for a big night. Lucky really. Not only do hangovers kill your workout intensity, they

also lower protein synthesis by 20%- twenty percent! And they're a massive waste of calories. Thank God I didn't need that kind of escape, Bec and I had a transparent relationship.

Bec enters transfixed on her book.

New Years Eve we partied at Jay's parents, then a hangover of more exams for Bec and a packed gym had me wishing January away. Bec was swamped with work so our brief lunchtime meets became key.

WILL   Close your mouth dear.

Will taps her mouth shut. Bec frowns. Will scrolls through his phone.

BEC   (*Hands Will his tupperware box*) Here. Carbs 31, protein 43, fat 14, taste 0.

Bec offers her cheek for a kiss.

WILL   Smashed it. Can you take a picture of my back?

Will hands Bec his phone and flexes his back.

BEC   Will!

WILL   No one's around, quick.

BEC   Will. If you're going to sit with me / please.

WILL   This has to be the last exam.

BEC   Don't make me feel bad about this, I can't be left behind.

Bec notices Will's phone.

Who's she?

WILL   PT.

BEC   Hashtag making eggs, hashtag FitFam! Hashtag could my tits be anymore out in this top.

Will laughs.

BEC   I didn't say that.

WILL   She practically lives in the squat rack and...

Scrolls his iPhone.

loves a selfie.

BEC   Well you can talk! Mr. I can't get changed without taking a picture with my top off. When did that become a thing?

WILL   Progress pics. Oi don't be like that, you know it's all for you.

Bec tries to remove something from Wills hair.

Will flinches with a smile.

What are you doing?

BEC   There's some fluff.

Attempts to get it again, Will jolts away.

WILL   What are you doing- get off- stop it. It's cool, I'll get it.

Will rubs down the sides of his waxed hair.

BEC   You look fine Will. Give me a kiss. Come here!

Bec kisses Will.

BEC   Don't be getting too big now.

Bec Exits.

WILL   I'm well off that. I let myself down in February, frosty windows and warm sheets meant all I hit hard was the snooze button. To achieve your lifting targets, you need to be mentally, physically and emotionally on plan.

                   March was Bec's Birthday and I was right back on it. Impressively she made it last the whole month. Jay smashed it suggesting to get her Lululemon sweat pants, you don't have to work out to wear gym clothes and Bec looked incredible in them.

Bec Enters.

BEC   We're meeting at seven.

WILL   I thought it was eight?

BEC   No, we've had this booked in for ages, the table is eight, Carly, Damon and Jay will be there at seven for drinks.

WILL   I was going to do my arms.

BEC   You've had all day and you don't need more than an hour in there.

WILL	I'll have to shower after.
BEC	You can shower at the gym. Will, I mean this.
WILL	Okay.
BEC	…
WILL	Yeah, no you're right. It's cool, I can make it up. Sorry.
BEC	What are you thinking?
WILL	Nothing.
BEC	Missing one session won't hurt you. Remember that Will!

Bec Exits.

WILL I missed the drinks but honestly she loved her leggings.

You need to be consistent to maintain progress. It works on a ratio of 3:1. 3 months gains all lost in 1 month. You can't have any distractions.

Jay enters and approaches the squat rack. He mimes a 1 rep max squat, shaking, he is unable to complete.

JAY Hhhm… ARGHH.

With Wills help he re-racks the bar.

Thanks. I had it though.

WILL You usually smash 8's out of this.

Will does squats in the rack.

JAY	Not feeling it.
WILL	Have some nitro bomb.
JAY	What's that?
WILL	Pre workout, 3 coffees in two scoops.
JAY	That stuff gives me the shits.
WILL	Have an Imodium chaser.

Will planks between sets. Jay sits down deflated.

What's up, you alright? Decided to wax your balls?

If it's an angle issue, I'm not helping!

JAY	Messed up haven't I?
WILL	What've you done?
JAY	Carly found out about a girl I pulled in Oceana.
WILL	Which one?
JAY	Oh don't say it like that. Monica, the Brunette Bob.
WILL	I can't keep up.
JAY	She had an inkling and jumped on it, had to tell her.
WILL	She find a text or condom?
JAY	Facebook.

Will laughs.

47

Don't mate.

WILL   Has she chucked you?

JAY   Touch and go. It's shit me up a little to be honest. I've not seen her cry like that since her Grandad passed. Bloody horrible, she just laid on the floor, weeping. Like really really upset.

WILL   I've never seen Bec cry.

JAY   Don't mess her about then.

WILL   I wouldn't.

Jay throws Will a look.

I wouldn't! Chat shit, got banged though init!

JAY   Fuck mate, I was hoping for a bit of support.

Will hands Jay a phone to film his next set.

WILL   Video this.

Will resumes working out.

JAY   What's this for?

WILL   Instagram, it's a good progress checker.

Will finishes the set and is back to plank.

With free reign maybe you'll hit the magic 7.

JAY   Nah… None of that. I need to chill out, make some effort.

WILL   That's a great idea of hers- I mean yours.

JAY	Right.
WILL	You'll both be fine, you always are. Spot me.

Will undertakes a final set of 3 reps.

JAY	If Carly or Bec asks; I've come here, poured my heart out, had a little cry and generally been a right mess yeah? And that I've only ever done this once! Just the one time.
WILL	Does she actually believe that?
JAY	It's the shaved chest, what can I say?
WILL	Leg raisers?
JAY	I'm done, I'm bloody useless here. How're you set for work?
WILL	Fine, why?
JAY	Over the bank holiday our Acton office needs a lick of paint. I'm sure they'll pay higher end.
WILL	Next weekend?
JAY	Yeah.
WILL	I'm ok.
JAY	Already working?
WILL	Yeah, here and there.
JAY	Ok well if it changes. Come on! Stop slacking, keep this up you'll be on the posters next.

Jay Exits.

WILL	I'm miles off that.
	It's important to keep track of your progress, to push back the goalposts. Remember you're always a work in progress.
	Disappointingly Jay disappeared with all the New Year new me gym goers. I thought he was stronger than that.

Bec Enters.

BEC	Why didn't you take the work Jay offered?
WILL	(*Beat*) Don't worry about me.
BEC	I do worry Will, having an 8 pack won't pay your rent-
WILL	I haven't got an 8 pack!
BEC	How much would you have earnt?
WILL	Depends. Quality workmanship takes longer than people think.
BEC	Roughly, five hundred? Because Dad said he'll pay six as he wants the kitchen done before Sunday.
WILL	What's Sunday?
BEC	We've got the family round, I told you?
WILL	Right, yeah.
BEC	Nanna, Grandad, Mum's cousins, they're looking forward to meeting you.
WILL	Great.

BEC	So will you do it?
WILL	What?
BEC	The work?
WILL	I'll think about it.
BEC	What!

Beat

	I thought you'd be pleased?
WILL	What do you mean?
BEC	...Well, unless you're cashing in loyalty points at the gym you've not earnt much lately, have you?
WILL	Not having a steady job doesn't mean I'm not working hard.
BEC	This isn't about the... forget it.

Will abruptly pulls Bec round.

WILL	No, go on?
BEC	You need to either get back to finding your own work or sign up with some agencies.
WILL	And not be in charge of my own time, no chance.
BEC	Ok forget the kitchen, please Will, you'll come right?

Bec goes to stroke his hair.

WILL   (*Will flinches.*) Sorry- love you.

Bec Exits.

I'd everything sorted. 8 long shifts a month, covered rent, gym, gym kitchen order. £100.00 on supplements. A new tee shirt and maybe a trip to the cinema. I should have questioned her, an ever closing diary had me sharing lunchtime meets with that friend.

Bec and Damon enter.

DAMON   Hello Mr Will, Mrs Bec.

Damon kisses Bec on both cheeks, then shakes Will's hand.

(*To Bec*) I signed for this at reception for you.

BEC   Thanks.

Bec passes Will the box.

WILL   Thanks.

DAMON   Get me a present did you?

Will excitedly opens the parcel.

WILL   (*Firm*) No.

DAMON   What is it?

BEC   It's his hulk juice.

Will and Bec share a smile.

DAMON   Ohhhh, cheating hey?

WILL   No! They're standard supplements.

DAMON	Looks pricey! What's that bottle for?
WILL	(*Reluctantly*) Green tea extract, it speeds up your metabolism.
DAMON	Cool, and the black tub?
WILL	BCAA's... Exercise causes an increase in serotonin levels, which causes fatigue. So BCAA's, branch chain amino acids, reduce these levels, which enhances your performance. (*Growing with enthusiasm*) And this bad boy is creatine, it improves recovery rates.
DAMON	Ever taken M.B's?
WILL	What are they?
DAMON	I read that all the big lifters do? I've got some M.B's with me actually, I'll give you some.
WILL	Right?

Damon, pulls his hand from his pocket and opens an empty palm out.

DAMON	Magic. Beans. I could earn a fortune at his gym.

Damon snorts with laughter.

BEC	Damon, I'll meet you there.
DAMON	Only joking Will mate, I'm jealous really. (*To Bec*) Skinny flat?
BEC	Please.

DAMON   Bye Will.

Damon Exits.

BEC   If you get to know him, he's actually quite
                   funny.

Silence

                   I've really got to go... We're all going for a
                   curry tonight, come with us?

WILL   ...I can't.

BEC   Brown rice, some veg, spinach! Bring your
                   fucking scales if you have to.

Bec Exits.

WILL   As the days got longer so did my sessions.
                   Busy bars meant empty gyms. Every day
                   they aren't training, I was doing a double!

Jay enters, catching Wills eye in the mirror.

JAY   Thursday evening, back and cardio?

WILL   Cardio was this morning. I'm surprised they
                   let you in without a membership.

JAY   I still come, you're just not here.

WILL   That belly tells a different story. Come on
                   then, watching won't help you.

Jay interrupts Will's exercise.

JAY   Wanna grab a coffee?

WILL   I've just had my pre workout.

JAY   Okay, I'll swing by in what, an hour, two?

Beat.

WILL   Come on spit it out.

JAY   Look at you hey. I gave you 2 months max, how wrong could I be?

WILL   Some want it more.

Will resumes his workout.

JAY   To think what you've achieved in a year is insane.

                       Puts me to shame.

WILL   Get back on it then.

JAY   You've got to admit you've changed alot from the Will who stepped in here last year.

WILL   You mean progress.

JAY   We just think, I just think maybe you need to take a week, recover a bit. You've no reason to be hitting it so hard.

WILL   I'm touched that you and Carly care so much/

JAY   And Bec.

WILL   I'm fine.

JAY   She's worried about you /

WILL   We're fine.

JAY   Well she isn't.

WILL   I've seen these on TV, interventions, this is the part where I break down and cry right?

Will heads to resume exercising but Jay stops him.

JAY   Okay. Your Mum was over for tea today, I hear your Dad's been back round giving her grief.

WILL   (*Firm*) Not in here mate. Not in here.

JAY   Course. Well if you want to chat, you know...

Jay Exits. Will bursts into exercise.

WILL   A steady routine. Nothing had changed, I didn't demand more or less of anyone. So how did I become the eye of the storm?

Bec Enters. Will is agitated and explosive. He sporadically pulls his top away from clinging to his chest.

BEC   Because you listen to him.

WILL   How do you think that makes me feel? Him thinking that you can't speak to me.

BEC   Stop it. The thing is, I don't know if I can.

WILL   (*Explodes*) Of course you can, what're you doing now!?

Will distressed, turns away from Bec.

BEC   Stop that! You're so distracted, Will, please look at me.

Bec touches Wills back. He flinches.

Bec Exits.

WILL   Why was everyone taking such an interest in how I lived my life? If it was too much drink, too many drugs, too much playstation or cholesterol, then yeah come and talk to me, but exercise. They needed to take a look at themselves.

I mean right now, my shoulders aren't in proportion to my triceps, this part of my bicep doesn't pertrude out, my upper chest has no definition, there's way too much fat around my waist so my transverse obliques aren't fully visible, my thoracolumbar has no strength, my traps are underdeveloped, uneven deltoids and don't get me started on my legs. So you can imagine the state I was in a year ago.

Nobody could find that attractive!

Bec and Damon Enter.

DAMON   Good Morrow Mr William.

Damon offers Will a nut.

Almond?

BEC   A what?

DAMON   An ALmond.

BEC   You mean an Allmond?

DAMON   Yeah. What? Yes an Almond, no Allmond, An Almond.

BEC   What are you doing? Allmond.

57

DAMON   Yes Almand /Allmond / Can I have an Almond. No wait-Almond an allmond.

Bec laughs, which makes Damon crack up.

Gosh. I don't really know what I'm saying, I'm not drunk at work promise! Almond, almond /

WILL   I don't want a nut!

Beat.

DAMON   No problem. Sorry. I'll see you back in the office. Will.

Damon Exits.

BEC   At least try to make an effort.

WILL   Make an effort!

BEC   He's a very good friend.

WILL   You're never more than 10 feet from one in London are you.

BEC   If you've got something to say, just say it.

Will notices her smoothie.

WILL   What's that?

BEC   Nothing.

WILL   Well it clearly is, what is it?

BEC   I'm on a juice diet.

WILL   What! Why?

BEC	I've put on a bit of weight since starting here.
WILL	No you haven't you look great. Anyway juicing's stupid. You like numbers, just calorie count, burn off more than you consume.
BEC	...
WILL	Why didn't you come to me for help? Is this Carly's idea? Don't listen to her you should want to be healthy not skinny.
BEC	God. Pot Kettle! The amount of tablets and powders you take /
WILL	Don't ask my opinion then.
BEC	I didn't Will!

Beat.

WILL	People only go on these stupid fad diets so they don't have to exercise. I'll write you a program, 12 week plan, 5 days a week, we'll sort your weight out in no time.
BEC	What?
WILL	I'll write you a plan.
BEC	Why are you doing this?
WILL	I'm 25 right? Which is where you scientifically reach your prime. Sexual peak is 18 so I'm already in decline. I just think we have this insane machine with unbelievable potential and while we can, we should push it to the max.

BEC	So you do think I should lose weight?
WILL	What! No, listen. Why do people run marathons or climb Everest? It's because they believe they CAN and that's a good a reason as any?
BEC	You're obsessed.
WILL	No, I'm focused.
BEC	Why can't you train like Jay?
WILL	He barely trains.
BEC	He does, and finds time for Carly.
WILL	Yeah and Sarah, Monica, Rachel, Holly.

Bec snaps.

BEC	Shut up!
WILL	What?
BEC	I said shut up!!

Beat.

WILL	You've heard that people only use 10% of their brain capacity right?
BEC	Jesus.
WILL	Wrong, myth. We use a 100% of it! You can achieve anything if you focus and push yourself.
BEC	Where are you Will?

WILL	I'm here.
BEC	Where's silly Will who'd order more wine at dinner?
WILL	I'm here.
BEC	And finish a tub of Ice cream.
WILL	New and improved-
BEC	Who goes out.
WILL	For you-
BEC	Has friends-
WILL	Bec-
BEC	Has fun?-
WILL	I've changed.
BEC	Why?-
WILL	For you-
BEC	What?
WILL	I changed for you!
BEC	(*Pleads*) Will.
WILL	You wanted Brad Pitt?
BEC	This is ridiculous.
WILL	It's what you wanted?
BEC	No it isn't.
WILL	You said you wanted Brad Pitt in fight club.

BEC	I don't want any of this Will.
WILL	Bit of a U turn.
BEC	I never have /
WILL	What do you want then?
BEC	I want to go back to work.

Will blocks Becs path.

WILL	No tell me now.
BEC	Let me go /
WILL	Tell me what you want!
BEC	What do I want? What do I want!? I want you to touch me, I want you to let me touch you. I want you to be more interested in my body than your own. To hold me and tuck my hair behind my ears like you used to. I want you to jump on me Will, to feel your breath in my ear, to fucking kiss me all over and love me. I want to get lost chatting about our future, or chatting absolute crap, because there is nothing that makes me happier, but now... now!

Remembering what they had and what they have potentially lost because of his obsession makes her turn on him.

	Do you really think your strength excites me? Turns me on? Makes me want you? Do think your limited chat stimulates anything in me?
WILL	Alright! I thought we we're fine?

BEC   Fine? Really? If we're fine.

Bec pulls a chocolate bar from her bag.

Eat this.

Please Will. Give me this.

Will doesn't move. Silence.

BEC   I'm done, you've done this. Remember that,
                 you've done this Will.

WILL   If you loved me you'd understand.

BEC   Loved you? If you love me you'll understand.

Bec Exits.

WILL   You know as a kid, you might be in a
                 restaurant or at a party and there are always
                 balloons. Now these catch your eye and
                 become the one thing you want more than
                 anything else in the whole world, nothing else
                 matters. If you're lucky- well as a kid you
                 usually get what you want, you get a balloon.
                 It's amazing, the right colour, shape. Once
                 you have it in your hand though, all you can
                 think about is what will happen if you let it
                 go, the curiosity of how losing it will make
                 you feel. So you let go of it. It's only at this
                 point of no return do you realise what it really
                 meant to you.

Will shakes off the memory.

I'd recommend the gym to anyone post break
up. Everyone's there to reflect and work on

themselves. Just like inside these four walls, we all want to get it done, get out there changed for the better.

I cancelled all work and tucked myself away at Mum's for a few weeks. Gyming late at night and steered well clear of mirrors. I hated what I saw so I had a lot of work to do.

Jay Enters.

JAY   Here he is.

Will continues in the zone.

You should bring your bed here, save you some time on the commute.

WILL   Join me or we'll chat after yeah.

JAY   I miss you man, how you been?

WILL   Body fats down 2% and making gains.

JAY   Well you're definitely the hardest worker in the room, no one can deny you that.

WILL   If you're not going to join me?

JAY   No worries. I'm not going to ruin your flow. Are you staying at the flat soon?

WILL   I've moved back to my Mum's.

JAY   Is she ok?

Beat

WILL	I gave in my notice last week. You've three weeks to find a replacement. I was going to text you.
JAY	What the fuck!
WILL	Sorry it slipped my mind.
JAY	Why wouldn't you tell me this? Jesus Will, they said you'd lost yourself in here but fucking hell.
WILL	Sorry?
JAY	Losing Bec mate what were you thinking?
WILL	Didn't work out.
JAY	Mate don't give me that.
WILL	Don't fucking "mate don't" me. You introduced me to the gym, "Bec will love it", "Be the hardest worker in the room".
JAY	I pulled you out of a pit. Sat around playing playstation, not leaving the house incase your Mum called you. This is all your choice.

Jay Exits.

WILL	Everyone in their mid-twenties are in such a rush to flee the nest, why? Free accommodation and less distractions equals more time to yourself.

Three months relentless training packed on some much needed mass, teamed with some nice attention round the gym, I felt ready to sample the fruits of my labour. |

65

Will undertakes each of the day's workouts slowly building pace and intensity.

Monday AM. Sweat out the turkey roast with fasted low intensity speed state. PM, my weakness, legs. Calf raises and compound squats get the body charged and the blood pumping. A recently changed topless Tinder pic meant the evening's plans were wrapped up. Amy a 19 year old blonde from Clapham. She was only my third ever lay so a 6/10 was excusable right? Luckily there aren't any pictures on a scorecard. So we go again.

Tuesday (*beat*) chest and tri's nice one. Focusing on it's upper definition I complimented it with a low V sweater. For the evenings entertainment I'd Elsie from the gym lined up, "couples that lift together, stay together". No chance, her hair smelt of the gym floor. And so we go again.

Wednesday, legs. You don't get second day DOM's, delayed onset of muscular soreness, if you rip them again. Luckily Sophie from reception loved it on top so no need to open my groin. Nice girl but she was already seeing one of the PT's, zero respect means we have to go again.

Thursday AM. I peel my head off the pillow for two hours of High Intensity Interval Training. Three days in a row was good innings. The evenings hunting attire was to be my favourite short sleeved Ben Sherman shirt, so that evening I trained my back, paying close attention to my lats; my wings, which helps any shirt hang well. Christmas drinks season was now in full swing so I didn't have to stalk far from home to find my prey.

Will undertakes squats, observing his form.

While servicing the twenty year old PA from Kew, I caught myself coming in and out of shot of my wardrobe mirror. At full hip extension the fat around my hip was collecting... Needless to say I couldn't come. A faked migraine and an empty promise to do lunch averted suspicion. And so we go again.

Friday AM cardio and abs shredded any lasting image of fat from my mind. It's a different game on a Friday, you've competition, most girls are keen for a dance so you want your legs light and water retention low to get the abs popping.

Arms PM leaves you pumped and ready to pounce. Tonight is Tanya keen to meet at mine. Not wanting to soil my surroundings we settle on a cheap common ground Travelodge. Which answers whether I took her number. And so we go again.

Saturday legs and shoulders. A double helping of pre workout gets me lifting clean and jerks. Spent out from Friday work drinks, Saturday night gym girls are all single.

Australian Crossfit enthusiast Stacey had managed to dodge the temptation of getting wankered at a Walkabout, she didn't refuse at her place.

A six day streak, left me hungry. This is what Jay had mentioned- the magic seven and I wanted it bad. (*Passionate*) And so we go again.

Sunday's a day of rest. Not at this church! A week of pumps- a week of girls, achievable reachable.

(*Rhymed*) I contemplated whilst I (*beat*) debated, if what I'm doing is wrong.

Late twenties though it's my time to show- I'm pulling in my harvest.

Six girls out of sight, disappeared with the night.

Bec is now just a number.

And so we go again.
And so we go again.

AND SO WE GO AGAIN!

Three scoops of nitro bomb and a can of diabetes, has me tearing through the gym door. Disgusted by my reflection, I punish my whole body.

Zero rest, a test of months and months of sculpting.

Beat.

That my decisions have been just.

Beat.

The finisher.

Will undertakes all the weeks exercises.

I run through the whole week in one workout.

Monday.
Tuesday.
Wednesday.
Thursday.
Friday.
Saturday.
Sunday.
Sunday.

Will crumbles. His breathing erratic.

I laid on the gym floor. Bec's face collating in the spots on the ceiling.

Jay enters and rushes over to will.

JAY   Will. Will!?

WILL   Jay.

Jay grabs Wills drink.

JAY   Have some water.

Disorientated.

Sit up, sit up Will, what are you doing?

Jay assists Will.

> Steady.

WILL   I didn't have breakfast. Silly really.

JAY   Over done it a bit. You ok?

WILL   Yeah.

JAY   Yeah?

WILL   I'm fine.

Will slowly regains his composure.

JAY   Keep sipping it.

WILL   I'm fine.

Beat.

> How come you're here?

JAY   Good job I am.

WILL   What do you want?

JAY   I bumped into your Mum in Tescos. She asked me to check on you and I knew you wouldn't answer my texts. She seemed well?

WILL   She is.

JAY   Good.

WILL   How are you?

JAY   Estate agent, work of the devil. Apart from that, not bad.

WILL   Good.

JAY   I hear you've been a busy boy?

Will looks across the room.

JAY   You always wanted someone who had abs.

Will locks eyes with Jay.

                 Can you stand?

WILL   Yeah.

JAY   Maybe call it a day.

WILL   I'm pretty much done. Thanks for popping in though.

                 If you want putting through your paces anytime.

JAY   I'd never keep up.

Jay is torn.

                 How are you set for New Years?

Will doesn't respond.

                 Same as always, parents place, you're more than welcome. Bring Mrs Motivator as well if you want.

Beat.

                 Wanna get a baggie in?

WILL   No!

They laugh. Jay Exits.

That's the beauty of friendship, however much time has passed you can just pick up right where you left off... Jay's seen it all.

Mum left Dad over two years ago. He just sat around and watched her leave. No fight. This "slut" he now calls her was the best thing that ever happened to him and he just watched her walk away. Now the fat lump of shit sits in a bedsit pickling himself.

I'm proud of my Mum for that, for walking away. Sad thing is I know she still wants him to fight for her.

New Years was five months since I last saw Bec, yet she'd been in every workout since.

That evening I was anxious to head out, excessively hitting my legs had neglected my upper body. So I doubled a chest tri's bi's and back sesh and made sure my hair was just right.

I was stronger now and there's nothing like a new year to start afresh.

Will enters the party.

Jay enters in an electric spirit, he is elated to see Will.

JAY   I said you'd come. Yes, good to see you man.

            It's gonna be a banger. You want a line?

WILL   No. I'm good.

JAY   Bec's here.

72

WILL   That's fine, times a healer, a bit like DOM's.

JAY   Ok. Well if you want some come find me. Train hard, party harder right?

Jay Exits.

WILL   It seemed like the whole of our School was there, people I haven't seen in years. I darted to the bathroom to check my hair- then back into the kitchen for a drink.

Bec Enters.

BEC   Will.

WILL   Bec!

Beat.

They hug

BEC   Jay mentioned you might come.

WILL   You know how persuasive he can be.

BEC   You look well.

WILL   Thanks, you too. Sorry do you want a drink?

BEC   What is there?

WILL   It looks like you can have... anything!

Bec Exits.

WILL   The hug was so familiar, warm and comforting. My body said leave.

Beat.

But I stayed.

Will is very uneasy in his surroundings.

I stuck to the room's perimeter, soaking in the atmosphere.

Then as the evening progressed I started to relax.

Jay enters, paranoid.

JAY Mate, take the coke. Carly's on to me. She'll go ape shit. I'll get it later.

Jay hands Will a baggie and he exits.

Will gains momentum.

WILL Eight o'clock became nine, one Tequila became two Sambuccas. I'd not felt like this all year, the party was kicking off!

The following grows, becoming jarring, heightened and disorientating.

I always knew where Bec was and we'd occasionally steal a glance across the room.

Beat.

Then one held look became a smile and I noticed she'd been wearing her hair up how I always liked it.

Beat.

Then Damon entered.

BEC He's a good guy.

JAY   Chat shit get banged.

WILL   I lost them into the crowd as my head pulsated, throbbing with the beating of the bass.

JAY   Chat shit get banged.

WILL   I stumbled into the kitchen to get some water

BEC   Damon's been great though.

WILL   I staggered out to join the crowds.

JAY   How do you know she isn't nailing her work mate?

BEC   Damon.

Damon Enters.

DAMON   You look absolutely stunning.

WILL   Damon!

Will circles them both.

My body bubbled with tension and I looked away. I was pissed, confused.

Uneasy in his footing.

The room swirled, my eyes erratic.

Will steadies his sight on Damon leaning towards Bec.

I tried to steady my breath as they merged into one.

Will charges at them both. A brutal attack.

BLACKOUT

Lights flicker on Will centre stage, staring at his hands. Sobered.

WILL   I guess I was a lot stronger than I thought. I have quite the Tyson right hook.

Mimes a fake right hook. He stops his stop watch.

58 minutes. That's a PB.

Will puts on an aluminous yellow vest.

I'm 2 months in now and I'm happy to say my heads a lot clearer than then. Annoyingly I got twelve, but keeping my head down I should be out in six.

Learning to cook as well which Mum likes. She pops by once a week. I've not heard from my Dad, but that's alright.

Right, off to see Jay. I wonder what he'll have to say?

Jay Enters. The following brings the action into the present day.

Will breaks the deathly silence.

WILL   Back on the weights I see, you look good mate.

Will joins a stoney Jay who's already seated.

Silence.

WILL   How's Carly?

Silence.

Do you want some water? The service is a little slow, but it's always done with a smile.

Will clicks his fingers.

JAY   I didn't know what I'd think when I saw you.

WILL   Not going to tell me you love me are you? Enough closet gays in here to be dealing with.

JAY   Why are you making a joke of this? Do you not have anything to say?

WILL   Mate. You came to see me!

JAY   Yeah.

WILL   What would you like to hear then Jay?

JAY   ...I don't know.

WILL   Okay. Well, I'm not a mind reader, so let me know if it comes to you yeah?

JAY   I'm gonna go.

WILL   Really? I've missed table tennis for this.

Jay gets up to leave.

               How's Bec?

Jay stops.

               She didn't come to the sentencing, I thought she might have. Guessing she's ok yeah? I hope so.

JAY   I'm not gonna talk to you about Bec.

WILL	Ok. Well, how's Carly?

Beat.

> Please mate, stay another five, It's nice to see you... Don't make me beg.

Jay takes a moment, then returns to sit in front of Will.

JAY	Carly and I aren't together anymore. Ended pretty soon after New Years.
WILL	Oh I'm sorry. You were good together.
JAY	Were we?

Silence

WILL	You still in the flat?
JAY	I've moved home for a bit.
WILL	Oh ok. Must be nice to see your Mum and Dad more.
JAY	(*Perplexed*) I guess so. (*Silence*) You aren't sorry are you?
WILL	For What? Turns out I was right about Damon! Him liking Bec.

Beat.

> Always was good at Cluedo.

JAY	Bec hasn't been herself since that night and Damon's face, fractured cheekbone, broken nose, two operations and God knows how many stitches. Really! Nothing?

WILL   Of course I'm sorry, I'm not an idiot. But I also know when I'm in the right.

JAY   Will you're in prison!

WILL   Bec getting in the way like she did. It's unfortunate, but we'll get through this.

JAY   It's time to let it go. Let her go.

WILL   I get what you're trying to say. Bec's with someone else now then?

JAY   What! How have you got that from what I've just said? She isn't with anyone!

WILL   (*Stands. Instantly becoming less personal.*) Thanks for coming in Jay, it's been good to see you. I hope you don't mind if I rush back, but I can still make it in time for the last of the round robins.

Jay makes to leave. Turns back.

JAY   Will. Please, get some help.

Jay Exits.

Will throws his yellow bib on the floor.

WILL   She isn't with anyone. I knew she wouldn't be, I don't know why I needed reassuring.

So 225 training days to get into the best shape possible.

One thing all this has shown me is the gym remains and I owe it a lot. In here people romanticise about how they're finding

79

themselves in solitude or achieving inner peace through Religion. Well I'm helping myself out with hard work. When down and out you can go one of two ways. Crumble and let it eat you whole or do what I'm doing, come out crunching.

A steely determination.

After all, if you're in shape, people notice you and being ignored is the last thing you want to happen.

BLACKOUT.

THE END

BODY DYSMORPHIC DISORDER FOUNDATION

What is BDD?

* Criticising and worrying about the way part of your body looks
  (but not mainly about being thin enough or worrying about becoming fat)
* Spending a lot of time (more than an hour) thinking about appearance every day
* Checking or 'fixing' appearance (e.g. checking in the mirror or other reflective
  surfaces, grooming activities, or skin picking)
* Hiding, covering, or disguising a perceived flaw in appearance
  (e.g. with make-up, hats, bulky clothes, or body posture)
* Comparing your appearance to that of other people
* Avoiding places, people, or activities because of your appearance concerns
  (e.g. bright lights, mirrors, dating, social situations, being seen close-up)
* Appearance related critical thoughts that cause a lot of anxiety & shame
* Interference with work, school, family, socialising, or relationships
  because of your appearance concerns

* BDD is not a product of the media
* About 1 in 50 people (or 2% of the population) suffer from BDD
* Almost as many men as women suffer from BDD
* The most common age at which people develop BDD is 13
* The cause of BDD is unknown, but it is associated with
  childhood abuse, bullying & teasing
* Any part of the body can be a focus in BDD
* The top areas of concern are nose, hair & facial skin
* Each year, 1 in 330 people diagnosed with BDD commit suicide
* BDD is a treatable condition
* Despite its seriousness, there is virtually no funded research into BDD
* Despite its seriousness, there are virtually no specialist clinics for BDD

W www.bddfoundation.org   **f** BDDFoundation

🐦 @BDDFoundation   **P** BDDFoundation

e info@bddfoundation.org

The Body Dysmorphic Disorder Foundation Registered Charity no 1153753